LET'S GET SILLY!

Nifty Knock-Knock Jokes

BY CAITIE MCANENEY

over 20 jokes!

HEHE!

KNOCK KNOCK!

WHO'S THERE?

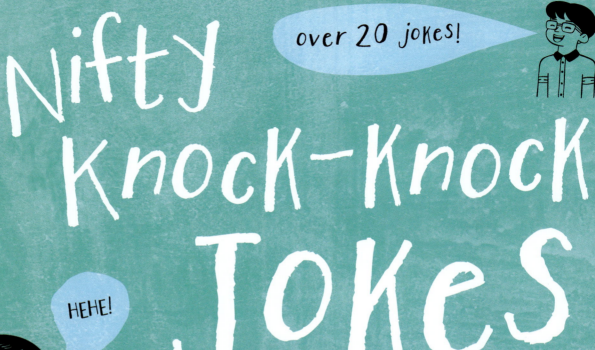

WINDMILL BOOKS

Published in 2025 by Windmill Books, an Imprint of Rosen Publishing
2544 Clinton St., Buffalo, NY 14224

Copyright © 2025 by The Rosen Publishing Group, Inc.

All rights reserved. No part of this book may be reproduced in any form without permission in writing from the publisher, except by a reviewer.

First Edition

Editor: Caitie McAneney
Book Design: Claire Zimmermann

Photo Credits: Series art (cover and interior illustrations) Huza Studio/Shutterstock.com; cover and interior (blue painted background) elena_l/Shutterstock.com; cover, p.1 (boy at top right corner) jesadaphorn/Shutterstock.com; cover, pp. 1, 18 (knocking hand) RetroClipArt/Shutterstock.com; series art (interior biege background paper) Q3kiaPictures/Shutterstock.com; p. 5 AI Generated/Shutterstock.com; p. 7 Helen lv/Shutterstock.com; p. 8 (owl illustration) cipta studio/Shutterstock.com; p. 8 (cow illustration) Polina Tomtosova/Shutterstock.com; p. 9 Sebastian Knight/Shutterstock.com; pp. 10, 11 (mustache illustrations) Only _up/Shutterstock.com; p. 11 (main) Viktoriia Hnatiuk/Shutterstock.com; p. 12 (tissue box) KatyaNesterova/Shutterstock.com; p. 13 Sv Svetlana/Shutterstock.com; p. 15 Bert e Boer/Shutterstock.com; pp. 16, 17 (hearts) Tube Lightt/Shutterstock.com; p. 17 Lisa Thomas Photos/Shutterstock.com; p. 19 Roman Samborskyi/Shutterstock.com; p. 20 (bee) kichikimi/Shutterstock.com; p. 21 Daniel Prudek/Shutterstock.com.

Some of the images in this book illustrate individuals who are models. The depictions do not imply actual situations or events.

Library of Congress Cataloging-in-Publication Data

Names: McAneney, Caitie, author.
Title: Nifty knock-knock jokes / Caitie McAneney.
Description: Buffalo, NY : Windmill Books, [2025] | Series: Let's get silly! | Includes index.
Identifiers: LCCN 2024023488 (print) | LCCN 2024023489 (ebook) | ISBN 9781538397930 (library binding) | ISBN 9781538397923 (paperback) | ISBN 9781538397947 (ebook)
Subjects: LCSH: Knock-knock jokes–Juvenile literature.
Classification: LCC PN6231.K55 M33 2025 (print) | LCC PN6231.K55 (ebook) | DDC 398/.7-dc23/eng/20240626
LC record available at https://lccn.loc.gov/2024023488
LC ebook record available at https://lccn.loc.gov/2024023489
Manufactured in the United States of America

CPSIA Compliance Information: Batch #CWWM25. For further information, contact Rosen Publishing at 1-800-237-9932

Contents

Knock Knock! 4

Furry Friends 6

Wild Fun 8

Just Plain Corny! 10

Silly Sounds 12

Jokes with Attitude 14

A Little Love 16

The Name Game 18

Just to Bug You 20

Glossary 22

For More Information 23

Index 24

Words in the glossary appear in bold
the first time they are used in the text.

Knock Knock!

Knock-knock jokes are some of the first jokes kids learn. They follow a simple **script**.

Knock knock.

WHO'S THERE?

Usually what's there is something very silly! The answer may **rely** on wordplay. It may also rely on the **element** of surprise.

Read on to learn some nifty knock-knock jokes!

Furry Friends

Knock knock. WHO'S THERE? Alpaca. ALPACA WHO? Alpaca the lunch, you pack-a the picnic blanket!

Knock knock. WHO'S THERE? Hugh. HUGH WHO? Hugh's a good doggy?! Me!

Knock knock. WHO'S THERE? Poodle. POODLE WHO? Poodle little ketchup on that hot dog!

6

alpaca (left) and llama (right)

Fun Fact
Alpacas may look like llamas, but they are different. They are both part of the camel family.

Wild Fun

Knock knock.
WHO'S THERE?
Iguana.
IGUANA WHO?
Iguana come inside!

Knock knock. WHO'S THERE?
Who. WHO WHO?
I didn't know you spoke owl!

Knock knock. WHO'S THERE?
Cows go. COWS GO WHO?
Noooo, cows go "moo"!

HAHA!

8

Fun Fact

Cows **communicate** with people and with each other! For example, they **vocalize** when they are hungry or **stressed**.

Just Plain Corny!

HEH HEH!

Knock knock. WHO'S THERE?
Spell. SPELL WHO?
Okay—it's spelled W-H-O.

Knock knock. WHO'S THERE?
Mustache. MUSTACHE WHO?
I mustache you a question.

Knock knock. WHO'S THERE?
Nana. NANA WHO?
It's Nana your business who it is!

〜 Fun Fact 〜

Mustaches became popular during the late 17th century in Europe, probably because there was a tax on beards in Russia.

Silly Sounds

Knock knock.
WHO'S THERE?
Cash.
CASH WHO?
No thanks, I prefer almonds!

Knock knock. WHO'S THERE?
Itch. ITCH WHO?
Bless you!

Knock knock. WHO'S THERE?
Boo. BOO WHO?
It's just a joke. No need to cry!

Fun Fact

Many people say "Bless you" when others sneeze. Others say "Gesundheit" (geh-ZOONT-hyt), which wishes the person "good health" in German.

Jokes with Attitude

Knock knock. Who's there? Interrupting cow. Interrupting cow who—? —MOOOOO!!!!

HA!

Knock knock. Who's there? Wooden shoe. Wooden shoe who? Wooden shoe like to know!

Knock knock. Who's there? Says. Says who? Says me!

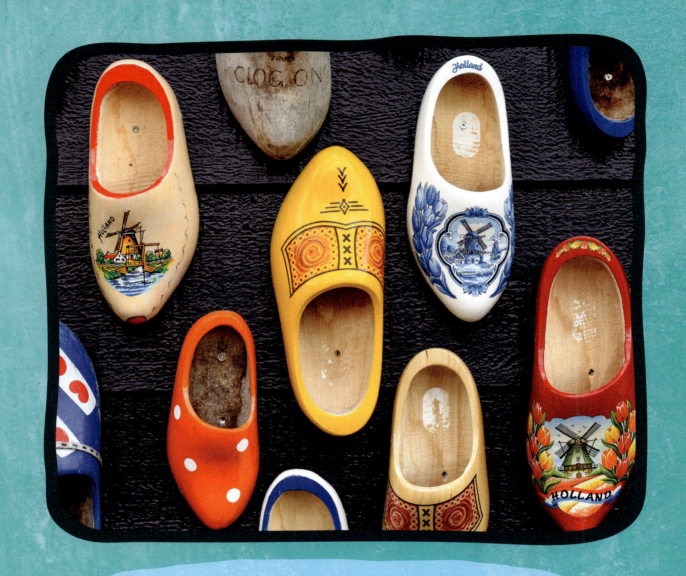

Fun Fact

Wooden shoes, also called clogs, date back to the Netherlands in the 13th century.

15

A Little Love

Knock knock.
WHO'S THERE?
Olive.
OLIVE WHO?
Olive you!
("I love you.")

Knock knock. WHO'S THERE?
Tank. TANK WHO?
You're welcome!

Knock knock. WHO'S THERE?
Heywood. HEYWOOD WHO?
Heywood you be my Valentine?

Fun Fact
Around 8 billion **conversation** hearts candies are produced every year for Valentine's Day!

The Name Game

Knock knock. WHO'S THERE? Norma Lee. NORMA LEE WHO? Normally, I just walk right in!

Knock knock. WHO'S THERE? Doris. DORIS WHO? Doris locked. Please open up!

Knock knock. WHO'S THERE? Ben. BEN WHO? Ben knocking all day!

TEEHEE!

18

:*. Fun Fact
Puns are a kind of wordplay that makes fun out of similar-sounding words and phrases.

Just to Bug You

Knock knock. Who's there? Honeybee. Honeybee who? Honey, be a dear and open the door!

Knock knock. Who's there? Amos. Amos who? A mosquito!

Knock knock. Who's there? Roach. Roach who? Roach you a text—didn't you see it?

Fun Fact

Honeybees are one of the most important animals for plants! They **pollinate** 80 percent of the world's flowering plants.

Glossary

communicate: To share thoughts or feelings by sound, movement, or writing.

conversation: Talk between two parties.

element: A basic part of any whole.

interrupt: To begin to speak before someone has stopped speaking.

pollinate: To take pollen from one flower, plant, or tree to another.

rely: To depend on something or someone.

script: The written text of a play, movie, or TV show.

stressed: Experiencing feelings of worry about something.

vocalize: To make sounds with the voice.

For More Information

BOOKS

King, Joe. *Knock Knock Jokes*. Minneapolis, MN: Abdo Kids Junior, 2022.

McAneney, Caitie. *Laugh-Out-Loud Animal Jokes*. Buffalo, NY: Windmill Books, 2025.

Panz, S. Marty. *The Giant Joke Book for Kids: A Silly Selection of Puns, Tongue Twisters, Knock-Knocks, and Animal Jokes!* Chicago, IL: Sequoia Children's Publishing, 2024.

WEBSITES

Just Joking-LOL
kids.nationalgeographic.com/videos/topic/just-jokinglol
If you like animal jokes, check out these funny videos from National Geographic.

Knock Knock Jokes
www.ducksters.com/jokes/knockknock.php
Explore lots of silly jokes from Ducksters.

Publisher's note to educators and parents: Our editors have carefully reviewed these websites to ensure that they are suitable for students. Many websites change frequently, however, and we cannot guarantee that a site's future contents will continue to meet our high standards of quality and educational value. Be advised that students should be closely supervised whenever they access the internet.

Index

alpacas, 6, 7

cows, 8, 9, 14

dogs, 6

element of surprise, 4

honeybees, 20, 21

interrupting, 14

mustaches, 10, 11

Netherlands, 15

pollinate, 21

puns, 19

Russia, 11

script, 4

sneeze, 13

Valentine's Day, 16, 17

wooden shoes, 14, 15

wordplay, 4, 19